good deed rain

Town in a Cloud

Allen Frost

© Copyright: 2015 Allen Frost
Good Deed Rain
Bellingham, Washington
ISBN 978-1-944242-39-8

Credits:
Production assistance: Fred Sodt
Writing and photos: Allen Frost
Apple by TFK!

If you have enjoyed this book
please share it with someone

BOOK 1: AIR TRAVEL

BOOK 2: OCTOBER WATER

BOOK 3: LIFE IN THE RAIN

Introduction:

LOTS OF RAIN passes through our town.
Once summer ends, we spend a good deal of
time with it. We may shut our doors and windows, but we invite it into our lives, we get to
know it, listen to it and are even inspired by it.
I thought these three little collections about rain
would make a nice book, a small book, the kind
that a traveler could carry, a book you would
have seen sold at bus stations or on those swiveling racks in drugstores.

AIR TRAVEL: Across the street from my bus
stop, there was a rowboat stood on end. The
sky was water. It looked to be waiting to row up
into air. So I decided to write a novel about it:
who was in it, where he went, fishing and being
fished.

OCTOBER WATER: Ever since I discovered
Santoka Taneda in his books *Mountain Tasting*
and *For All My Walking*, I felt a connection. I
wanted to travel with him. I haven't been to
Japan but it feels familiar, we have an inland sea
too and islands and fog, the same trees and rain.
I gave myself one month to write haiku inspired

by those wandering Japanese poet monks. These poems also take a similar journey, finally begging from door to door, a ritual that has another meaning at the end of every American October.

LIFE IN THE RAIN: This is almost a real life diary, an account of living through the wet Northwest spring, after all the rain of fall and winter, waiting for it to stop, waiting for the sun.

they built their town
inside of a cloud
living their lives
within it

Allen Frost
September 23, 2015
Bellingham, WA

AIR TRAVEL

Part 1: THE BROKEN FISH

Chapter 1
A boat stood on end, bow pointed at the sky.
Of course, this was how it got around, cast off
from the oak tree it leaned roped against
and up it went.

Chapter 2
The man who rowed rode it like a rocket,
vertical at first, then, past the electric wires
and above the rooftops, he leveled off,
scooping the oars hard into the air.

Chapter 3
Now he could look down peacefully
on the backyards and streets and trees.

Chapter 4
It all depends on what you're looking for.
This early morning, an old aluminum sky
before the sun fully shined, he rowed to the sea
to go fishing.

Chapter 5
He followed the road as it flowed
fifty feet below, slowly leading the way.
The oarlocks creaked with each pull.
A rooster crowed a few blocks away.

Chapter 6
Oh, sometimes he stopped rowing
and let the boat drift. There was no hurry,
holding the oars out flat like wings
nailed to a wooden bird.

Chapter 7
A chestnut tree brushed its leaves
along the smooth planks underneath,
a sigh as hushing as a seaweed bed.

Chapter 8
When the land gave way to water
he rowed a little further over waves
then pulled in the oars.

Chapter 9
He looked over the edge to see
the spot where the kelp fanned out.
Motoring in and out of there
like birds in trees, were salmon.

Chapter 10
Sooner or later one of them would see
the silver spark of light in the water
not knowing it was a sharp hook
connected to a line traveling up
forty feet into the sky.

Chapter 11
He watched his reflection
that other him leaning over
in an upside down boat
fishing at the sky.
Connected by the same line
he was fishing for himself.

Chapter 12
Then the line twitched.
His reflection caught something
in the deep cloudy sky.

Chapter 13
He caught a rockfish.
It was stripes and spines
spinning its fins in the air.
He pulled it twenty feet
from the water to the boat.

Chapter 14
"Oh great…" the fish said
when it got to him.

Chapter 15
This part was never easy.
Since animals started talking
everything had changed.

Chapter 16
He took the hook out,
telling the fish, "Look…
I hate to do this to you…"
"Sure you do," the fish replied.
"*You* hate it. How do you think I feel?"

Chapter 17
The fish was kept in a bucket
with seaweed packed around.
It griped for a while, until
it became hard to breathe.

Chapter 18
About five minutes later
the man caught something else.
It flapped against the water like an umbrella

Chapter 19
He knew what it was.
Anyone who fished these waters day after day
once in a while caught a sea parrot by accident.

Chapter 20
Sea parrots wouldn't try for hooks.
They were said to be too smart for that.
It was bad luck that caught it and
bad luck for those who caught them.

Chapter 21
Talk about talk!
It was like a radio
on the end of a hook.

Chapter 22
Back in the old days
before animals could talk
it was easy to kill a fish.
Just hit it with a stick.

Chapter 23
Now you had to listen to their sad life story.
Some of them could really lay it on thick.
Still, if he let them all go, he wouldn't eat.
It was a predicament.

Chapter 24
He contemplated cutting the line
letting the sea parrot go free.
But even that could bring trouble.
Word gets around.

Chapter 25
A sea parrot can carry a grudge
track you down in the shallows
when you least expect it.
Being a fisherman means
accepting certain risks.

Chapter 26
The sea parrot didn't waste any time.
The man knew it wouldn't.
The moment he got it aboard,
the fish wagged its yellow fin,
showing him the hook pinned to it.

Chapter 27
"Do you have any idea how this feels?!"
The man sighed. He didn't want that fish.
Anyway, they weren't good eating.
They were all mouth.

Chapter 28
Some people kept them for companions.
Maybe he could try selling it in town.
He had seen them in jars and pans
playing the water like calliopes.

Chapter 29
He didn't want to start a conversation though.
He lay the fish on the bench and kept it flat
took hold of the hook and twisted.

Chapter 30
"You're a maniac!" the fish screeched.
It paddled the air lamely. "You broke my fin!"

Chapter 31
The man pictured the ocean listening.
"Just keep it down," he said. "Don't yell."
"Don't yell?!" The fish sat up and gaped.
"You're trying to kill me!"

Chapter 32
"No," he said, flustered. "Look…
I'll put you back." The man tried
to scoop the sea parrot off the bench.

Chapter 33
"Oh no you don't! I can't return like this!
You have to fix my fin!"

Chapter 34
It was true, the man knew it.
An angry sea parrot could ruin him.
In no time at all, the sea would be
a newspaper. Every shrimp, crab
and whale would know the story.

Chapter 35
If that happened, he would have to
row his boat to a desert somewhere
and make a living sifting sand.

Chapter 36
"Okay!" the man said. "I'll take you home
I'll repair your broken fin." He carefully
lifted the sea parrot and put it into the bucket
pulling some seaweed over to protect it
from the overcast light of day.

Chapter 37
"Wait a minute!" the fish brayed.
"Someone's already in here!"

Chapter 38
"Oh yeah…I forgot," the man said.
The rockfish gave a cough and rasped,
"Don't mind me. I'm just a forgotten fish
left in here to die…"

Chapter 39
The sea parrot leaned out of the bucket
and shrieked at the man, "What is the
matter with you? You've got to get this
poor fellow back in water right away!"

Chapter 40
It was no surprise really
all the fish noise attracted a seagull.
It landed on the bow
on the little triangle of wood.
It blinked yellow eyes and
dipped its smooth white head.

Chapter 41
"That was supposed to be my lunch…"
the man said. The sea parrot choked,
"Lunch!?!" sweeping the weeds clear
from the wilting rockfish, "This fellow
probably has a family to support!"

Chapter 42
"I do," the rockfish wheezed.
"Oh come on…" said the man.
The sea parrot wagged a fin at him,
"Imagine not being able to see your
loved ones because some barbarian
fed you a steel hook and threw you in a pail.
It's criminal!"

Chapter 43
"Don't I know it!" sobbed the rockfish.
He gave a feeble twitch. The sea parrot
commanded, "Go on, return him!"

Chapter 44
As the rockfish flipped and glittered
through the air, the seagull yelled
and dove after the splash.

Chapter 45
"There goes my lunch," said the man.
The sea parrot shrugged. He was
philosophical about it.

Chapter 46
There wasn't much point lingering
in the air. The man knew it.
He stowed his fishing rod and
pushed the oars out to row
back the way he had come.

Chapter 47
The water waved goodbye.
The town was awake by now,
little fires sent smoke out chimneys.
A dog barked up at him. He was
returning with a broken fish.

Part 2: INVISIBLE SPACE

Chapter 48
About a year ago he went to
The Invisible City. It wasn't much
to look at, you might not even know
it was there.

Chapter 49
From his boat in the air
it was trees and gardens
planted in lines and squares
with patches of dirt where
buildings were. Streets were
scratched into the soil.

Chapter 50
When he lingered over
a baseball diamond, the ball
would hit his boat sometimes.

Chapter 51
You could hear things happening below.
Maybe that would be a better name for it:
The City of Sound.

Chapter 52
He went there for bargains,
things he couldn't afford back home.
They had a different rate of exchange.

Chapter 53
Strange that he never tried fishing
in their lakes, rivers or streams.
Then again, what could he do
with an invisible fish?

Chapter 54
Anyway, a year ago or so
he bought a house there
and towed it back to the yard
where he parks his boat.

Chapter 55
Back then, when the house
settled down, crushing a big square
into the grass, he was a little worried.

Chapter 56
With a ladder, he went all around
the invisible corners of it, wrapping it
with a rope. It did look weird to see
a lasso in the air holding nothing.

Chapter 57
Then he hung flags, clothes and rags
so nobody would run into the house.
That also gave the house a sound,
when there was wind.

Chapter 58
But he didn't have to worry about
animals running into the house.
They seemed to know it was there.

Chapter 59
Birds would fly around it
bees would veer on their paths
to where the flowers were.

Chapter 60
For him, there were some things
to get used to—memorizing the rooms
the doorways and invisible stairs…

Chapter 61
Sleeping was easy though.
High off the ground, being in bed
the world around him would get dark and
it was just like floating along in his boat.

Chapter 62
Waking up was rough.
As soon as the night began to fade
into dawn, the sea parrot's voice
would turn on like an alarm.

Chapter 63
"Albert!...Mister Roselli!" He could
hear his name being thrown at him.
He was a floor away but it didn't matter.

Chapter 64
He opened his eyes. The day was
a dull colored clay. He had to get up.

Chapter 65
Yes, he thought of draping a cloth
over the fish tank, the way people do
with their canaries at night,
but the sea parrot wouldn't allow it.
It wanted natural light. It was an
early bird.

Chapter 66
And as long as it stayed in his house,
slowly mending, Albert couldn't go fishing.
He had to take another job to make ends
meet. He made origami. He got paid
by the swan.

Chapter 67
Albert had been making them for years.
It wasn't difficult work. He could make them
in his sleep. And it paid. Believe it or not
there was always a demand.

Chapter 68
So he was lucky to have this job.
After all, there couldn't be too many
people making an origami living.

Chapter 69
After he fed the sea parrot, Albert sat down
in the rocking chair. He pulled the blanket
over his legs and closed his eyes. Sometimes
the fish let him sleep for a while. He could
listen to the popping sound of the fish eating
and the creaking of the slow rocking chair
levitating in the middle of a dark early morning.

Chapter 70
While he was half awake, Albert also heard
the movement of something else. It was
prickly, like a ball of newspaper blown
gently across the floor.

Chapter 71
He had been aware of this sound in the house
the sound without a visible source, he could
only assume it was a ghost. His invisible house
was haunted.

Chapter 72
After sharing the house with Albert for weeks
(relaxing like a television image in a pool of
clear sea water that Albert replaced twice a day)
it took this quiet October morning for the fish
to finally notice the ghost too.

Chapter 73
"Albert!"
Albert opened his eyes.
"What's that noise?" the fish cried.
Albert sat and listened to the ghost
turning pages.

Chapter 74
"There's a spook in your house!"
"Yes," Albert told the fish, "I know."
And then something miraculous occurred.
The fish chimed, "I want out of here!"

Chapter 75
On the journey back to the sea,
the fish went on and on about it.
"That's one thing we don't have to
put up with in the ocean. No ghosts!
The tide takes care of them
and washes them away."

Chapter 76
The October wind was picking up and
it was hard rowing but even the cold blowing
couldn't drown out that fish's talking.

Chapter 77
Albert stopped in the same place
that used to be lucky for him,
the bed of brown kelp leaves.

Chapter 78
The sea parrot was back in the bucket
waving its fins. It ripped off its little white cast
—that's how much a hurry it was in.
Albert lifted the bucket by rope and began
to lower it hand over hand.

Chapter 79
The sea parrot was going in reverse,
taking the exact opposite journey
on a line back to the water, hopefully
for forever.

Chapter 80
Albert let the bucket sink into a wave.
He could see the fish flap out and blur
into the murkiness and gone.
He pulled the fresh weight of water
back up again. It was heavy but to
Albert it felt so much lighter.

Chapter 81
In fact, upon returning to hovering over land
he descended quickly and parked his boat
beside a lamppost on the shore.

Chapter 82
He tossed the rope around the pole
and hopped out before a grocery store.
Five minutes later, he returned with daisies.
The white flowers were a present for the ghost.

Chapter 83
His house was fluttering all its big
and little sails on the invisible walls.
His blanket moved on the rocking chair,
though by the time he tied his boat
at the tree and turned to look again,
the blanket was folded still.

Chapter 84
He never had any trouble with the ghost.
He only noticed it passing a few times a day.
But sometimes he woke up at night and
he wondered if it was giving him dreams
when he saw places from long ago
where he had never been.

Chapter 85
He made sort of a big show as he entered.
"Hello!" he called. He shuffled in slowly like a
deep sea diver. "I brought you a present…
I want to say thank you…"

Chapter 86
Albert stopped in the kitchen and listened.
Nothing. He reached into an invisible cupboard
and took down a vase. He reached for the
invisible faucet on the invisible sink and filled
the vase with clear water.

Chapter 87
The house was still silent as he settled
the flowers into the invisible water
and held it up to the air.

Chapter 88
"I just wanted to say thanks.
You scared off that fish.
I guess it was getting on everyone's nerves…"
Nothing happened. "I don't know if you like
flowers. I don't know what ghosts like."

Chapter 89
Nearby, someone laughed and someone else,
closer to Albert said, "We're not ghosts."

Chapter 90
Albert stood there and listened to them.
"This used to be our house," said another unseen voice.
"We didn't want to leave," said a girl.

Chapter 91
"Ohhh," Albert said, figuring it out.
"You're from The Invisible City…"
Nearby, someone corrected him,
"It's only invisible to you."

Chapter 92
"You're not ghosts?" Albert stumbled on.
A laugh, "That's what you people call us."
From the sounds of their voices, there were four of them. Albert asked, "You're a family?"
"That's right," they said.

Chapter 93
Albert sat in his rocking chair. On the table where the fish used to be were the flowers. Outside, which was all around him, leaves were blowing, falling and swirling on the jagged grass, rain was hissing, the yellow trees were bending and waving.

Chapter 94
"I lost my job," Norman Withers told Albert. "We ran into some hard times. We lost the house. We had nowhere to go. What were we supposed to do? So we stayed with the house."

Chapter 95
"We didn't think you would notice us," said Doris. "We tried to be quiet." Her children were near her, Albert could hear them too.

Chapter 96
So there was an invisible family in his invisible house. Now that he knew, it was better. He let them have their rooms back. They could live the way they were used to.

Chapter 97
He tried to give them space.
He had a little room in the attic,
a bed and a light, creaking floorboards…
Basically, Albert Roselli became a ghost.

Part 3: THE BEES

Chapter 98
That went on for a while,
until one day about a year later,
the door opened and slammed
and feet ran across the floor.
In a second, everyone was yelling.

Chapter 99
Albert knew something was going on
so he went downstairs to find out.

Chapter 100
"We won a contest! We're going to Fiji!"
"What?" Albert stood there staring at the yard.
It was covered with a surprise of Halloween
orange and yellow leaves.

Chapter 101
Albert drove their invisible Pontiac.
They were all around him, excited and
talking over each other. He felt like
he was sitting in the air, driving off
the ramp onto the highway, moving
in between cars and trucks on the way
to the airport.

Chapter 102
It wasn't the airport he was used to.
They directed him out of town.
Trees grew close to the road.
The radio stopped getting a signal.
"This is our exit!" Norman pointed.
Albert saw a road diving into woods.

Chapter 103
Following Norman's directions,
Albert took them to an autumn field.
He parked the car next to a slumping
haystack of blackberry. The front tires
sunk into the soft ground.

Chapter 104
Albert stood there beside the invisible car
in a clearing. If it wasn't for the family,
he would have felt all alone. Only the stars
shrilled beyond the daytime of the sky.

Chapter 105
"Goodbye Albert!" they all sang.
He didn't know where they were
but he was used to the feeling.
It was like talking to himself.
"Goodbye," he said to the air.
"Have a good time."

Chapter 106
He might have heard propellers beating above.
The wind picked up, he couldn't be sure.
After a while, he felt behind himself
and found the invisible car again.

Chapter 107
He got back onto the seat,
held the wheel, turned the key
and he was on his way home.

Chapter 108
A blue truck was stopped in front his house.
Wooden boxes had fallen off the open tailgate,
the driver was standing there beating at the air.

Chapter 109
Albert parked the Withers' car in the driveway
and hopped out. Bees were whirring from their
broken hives, clouding the sidewalk.

Chapter 110
The truck driver had done all he could.
He couldn't get the bees back into the boxes
and he was getting stung standing there.
He jumped back in his truck and drove away
leaving a cloud of bees.

Chapter 111
Albert knew it was way too cold for bees
to be buzzing around out of doors. Plus,
there were no more flowers this time of year.
It was going on winter.

Chapter 112
So he strolled up to that bee cloud
and asked if they wanted to follow him.

Chapter 113
At first it was like leading a bristling
black and yellow tiger. Once they got
inside, the heat was on, and he showed
the bees to his rocking chair. "Here," he said,
"Make yourself at home."

Chapter 114
The bees climbed onto the chair
and sat down in a big soft shape
purring one buzzing word, "Warmmmm…"

Chapter 115
It took Albert about an hour in town
going through the big market buildings
and warehouses, checking the alleys
and loading bays too, before he found
the perfect replacement beehives.

Chapter 116
He strung them together
in his rowboat and rowed home
like an orchestra.

Chapter 117
Like someone setting up for Mozart,
Albert carried them inside: a stack of violins,
most of a guitar, and a broken cello.

Chapter 118
He brought them downstairs to the cellar
where it was dark and it wasn't too cold
and it wasn't too warm and he hung up
their homes on the wall.

Chapter 119
The bees took to them right away
filling the musical instruments
with a sleepy hum.

Chapter 120
If nobody showed up for them,
if winter went by, Albert would
carry the beehives carefully out
to the backyard in the spring.

Chapter 121
He would put them in the new
green leaves. They could work
all the flowers in the neighborhood.

Chapter 122
And when their labors were done,
those hundreds of bees would unseal
their wooden seamed homes to reveal
musically shaped honeycombs.

Chapter 123
On one of those warm summer days
that felt so far away from now
they would begin to play
over beeswax and delicate strings.

Part 4: A POSTCARD

Chapter 124
The next week, Albert opened
the tin door of the mailbox.
He didn't see anything
but he reached in anyway.

Chapter 125
His hand touched the flat paper
shape of an invisible postcard.
He held it tightly, he didn't want
to drop it as he returned to the house.

Chapter 126
How were you supposed to read
something you couldn't see?
For a while, he tried all kinds of ways:
holding the card up to candlelight,
against shadows, sunlight, into steam…

Chapter 127
What did a postcard have to say anyway?
Not much. It probably just wished he was there.
Still, Albert wanted to know.

Chapter 128
Finally, he felt along the wall for the telephone.
He found it and held the receiver to his ear.
Everything belonging to the Withers family
remained invisible to him.

Chapter 129
Every once in a while, a chair or
a toy on the floor would knock him down.

Chapter 130
"Hello," Albert said. "I received a postcard
in the mail today, but I can't read it.
It's invisible."

Chapter 131
He listened to the voice on the other end,
miles away, connected by electricity,
someone in The Invisible City
telling him what to do.

Chapter 132
To be sure not to lose the postcard
in the meantime, Albert stuck the card
under a visible bowl of apples on a visible
table made from brown colored wood.

Chapter 133
The table stood upon an invisible floor
ten feet off the ground. So it seemed
Albert spent most of his time in the air.

Chapter 134
The Withers left canned food for him to eat
while they were gone. It was strange
never knowing what you had until
you tasted it.

Chapter 135
He was sitting in his rocking chair
making a red apple disappear when
he happened to see a flat cardboard box
floating towards the house.

Chapter 136
Albert waved, knowing
someone was carrying it
then he went to the door.

Chapter 137
When he got the cardboard open,
there was a book inside. Thankfully
it was a book he could feel and see.
Written on the cover was the title:
How To See Invisible Things.

Chapter 138
After the first sentence, Albert wondered
if it was such a good idea to keep reading.
It said, "Once you have read this simple
book of instructions, nothing will be
invisible to you ever again."

Chapter 139
What did that mean anyway?
Would he be in two worlds at once?
Or would everything he used to know
get replaced by what used to be invisible?

Chapter 140
He was afraid to read anymore.
Maybe it was too late, maybe
the world he knew was already fading.

Part 5: WHAT HAPPENED

Chapter 141
Albert left the book on the table
beside the fruit and went outside.
Of course it always seemed like he was
outside, but once he passed through
the doorway, he could feel the weather.

Chapter 142
Fortunately, it was sunny.
One of those crisp apple days
at the end of October.

Chapter 143
It still seemed like the same old reality.
A crow watched him leave the sidewalk,
onto the grassy path that led to the woods.

Chapter 144
There were a lot of orange leaves on branches,
also, a lot on the ground. The leaves were in
two worlds at once.

Chapter 145
As he crossed the little wooden bridge
into the forest, a tree above him shook.
An owl unfolded brown bark-looking wings
and soared quietly to another spot.

Chapter 146
The owl turned and stared at Albert
with two black eyes like windows at night.

Chapter 147
That was strange, Albert thought.
It was still a couple hours before sundown,
why would an owl be out in the day?
Hunger, he supposed. There were squirrels
and other meals walking around.

Chapter 148
Albert realized he didn't really have
a destination, he just went walking
to get away from that book.

Chapter 149
He stopped. The woods were awfully quiet.
Shadows were painted down from the trees.
He decided to cut through the field.

Chapter 150
He had to duck and bend around
the remains of an old barbed wire fence.
This used to be a farm, now it wasn't.
There were waves of flattened weeds.

Chapter 151
Albert Roselli felt like he could have been
the only one on the planet. The field was
framed all around by the winter trees.
He was in the middle, crunching across
wading in fog, passing a big blackberry
mound. It looked like a waiting bus.

Chapter 152
As he came around the bumper of thorns
and vines, another picture was waiting
frozen as a painting, or the scene from
a TV show before the music bursts.

Chapter 153
A deer, ears fluted out like flowers,
stared at Albert. They weren't alone.
Ten feet away was a lion.

Chapter 154
This was one of those times
Albert was thankful animals could talk.
The three of them had to figure out
something fast.

Chapter 155
"Hello…" Albert said.
The deer whispered a worry.
The lion moved to the side a little.
Albert took a step towards the deer.
The whole thing moved like something
pushed in the wind.

Chapter 156
The lion had a buttery voice
hot as an opened oven. "I'm hungry."

Chapter 157
The deer was still. It wanted to be a tree.
Albert stepped all the way in front of the deer
dreaming itself into bark and leaves.

Chapter 158
The trees were barely there anymore.
The fog was filling up everything.
Albert couldn't even see his feet.

Chapter 159
Albert told the deer to leave.
He hoped it would understand. It did.
Leaving him with his back to a wall of fog.

Chapter 160
It was like a black and white movie
they used to make. Only the lion
glowed in golden yellow color.

Chapter 161
The lion took a step and asked Albert,
"Why did you let my meal get away?"
Albert said, "It looked so scared."

Chapter 162
The lion took another step closer.
"Now what shall I eat?" it purred.
Albert said, "Me, I suppose."

Chapter 163
"You're not scared too?" the lion asked.
It was only a jump away. Albert said,
"No. I guess not. When I'm gone from here
 I'll be somewhere else."

Chapter 164
"Can you do me a last favor though?"
Albert asked. "Can you make it quick?"
He knew it could move like a rocket.
The lion smiled. "You won't even know
what happened."

OCTOBER WATER

October
one last dragonfly
over the lake

Ten years old
catching hands
on a falling leaf

The cold tree
standing in yellow leaves
holding onto green

Watching seagulls
white dots on the green
baseball diamond

Outfield marched
by the dots of slow
white gulls

This foggy morning
clouds too tired for sky
drag on the ground

This foggy morning
in and out of white
like meeting in the sky

Stop to read
the city today
an empty page

Somewhere
a raven calling
off in the fog

A break at work
I find old friends
poets of Japan

Walking along
mist on the hills
Basho poetry

Writing poems
a long meditation
traveling to the end

Now I can count
the flowers on this hill
seven dandelions

Another apple
chewed down
to the core

A bulldozer
stopped to eat
a pile of dirt

At 3 A.M
the haunted past
living on TV

Fog asleep
in a bed of trees
roused by sun

The steep hills
home to dragons
made of clouds

Enough wind
to push a leaf
on the bricks

A leaf sailboat
crosses the bricks

A leaf sailboat
for a moment
then like the others

Leaves in piles
paperwork
on my desk

A tree of moonlit plums
picked over by raccoons

With the moon
caught in its web
the spider sleeps

Going to bed
just to go back to work
a bad dream routine

On my lunchbreak
I watch hungry ants
surround a crumb

Missing the bus
on purpose
I walk home

The night bus
hear it pass the house
moving dreams about

Rainy night
tuned into the sound
Japanese poetry

Window open
only wide enough
for haiku

Voices carry
like radio waves
across from Japan

The long journey here
pares away the words
to only a few

Washed up on shore
hidden among
the stones and weeds

Try to find poetry
wherever you are

A crow
dropped onto
all that white sky

A crow
dropped onto
the empty sky

Awake early
catching the deer
standing in the garden

Loud crows
on a pine tree
shut up already!

In the woods
the leaves tell you
it's raining

All night long
the rain flows
around us

3:30 A.M calm
the rain is finally gone
so why am I awake?

Cold coyote
is there anyone else
awake to hear you?

From the shower
I hurry to write
another haiku

Trying to dry off
yesterday's rain
turns into today's

Wooden house
stacked like a boat
against the rain

All the rain
pours in drains
below the sidewalk

All that rain
rushing water
below the ground

Beside the curb
looking at the grate
listening to the river

A dead waxwing
tailfeathers daubed yellow
buried with a flower

Gray clouds today
small drops of rain
getting colder

The young tree
it looks afraid
to drop its leaves

October sun
bright and burning
in the leaves

Tomato soup
that's all I want
in my bowl

An eye for color
and beauty in the world
she carries a leaf

The garbage truck
hisses and sighs
down our street

An old woman
pushing the curtain
watches the bus go by

On the wet street
a rainbow follows each car

Parking lot acorn
the miracle of a tree
waiting in you

Countless cars
fill the road
like buffalos

Follow the signs
listen to the radio
Seattle will appear

It's hard to fit in
what kind of world is this
where is what used to be?

Life out of balance
even the deer are left
looking unreal

Just look around
what you see is only
projected like a movie

We're used to it
the floating bridge
we pay a toll to cross

At the Japanese market
daikon stacked like cordwood

Behind the fence
a moonlit Buddha
for sale

Old friend
3 A.M
back again

A lamp turned on
the tired house
wants to sleep

One light turned on
the house needs a while
to wake up

The air today
too much like water

Secretly
moss is growing
everywhere

A little boy
sings on the bus
until we notice

Beginning here
this space for walking
arriving over there

In the woods
don't forget
take a deep breath

The blue sea
shines through
the green of trees

Railroad tracks
sewn to the map
paper crackles

Everything is quiet
still as a photograph
waiting for the train

All the stones
between the rails
holding their breath

Our yellow dog
standing in the ocean
gives it a lap

I know the feeling
barefoot on barnacles
so I wear shoes

Those fir trees
stand in the rain
dark and crowded

Tell the rain
you don't mind
getting wet

These nonstop drops
diamond and diamond
the window again

Inside for hours
finally let outside
submarine weather

Those dark stones
placed in a stream
to walk across

I go back in time
without a machine
that path leads me there

Inside a dream
visit people, see the sights
other worlds

Our quiet room
only the ticking
bedside clock

A new dawn
clear enough to see
a few stars

Lying on the floor
her long dog nose pointed
at her empty bowl

Grocery cart parked
filled with belongings
he sits down

The homeless man
in the parking lot
feeding crows

A little blue sky
four seagulls fly by
in a row like buttons

Wind-up the wind
let it blow itself out

Only a few crows
urgent enough to fly
in this crazy wind

A sudden wind
makes all the leaves
run on the pavement

Dave interrupts me
and I forget the poem
so easily

He wants to know
do I want two snow tires
he found on the street?

This much tread is left
Dave holds up two fingers
like squeezing a penny

There's a reason
people leave things
on the side of the road

Yesterday
there was a puddle
in this spot

Lighter than air
the slow heron creaks
above the trees

Cars hurry in town
the mountain appears
white cold snow

Robert's house
down the alley
cedar and bamboo

A teacup
left outside
filled with rain

Rainy islands
ocean and sky
the same color

Smell the ocean
walking outside
to a gray sidewalk

By slow degrees
the sea gets closer
cold, wet air

Swans flying south
the rising sun lights them
from below

Rain on my back
pulling out the stalks
dead summer flowers

Three weeks of rain
the gutters are full
water spills out

It's still raining
a long voyage
from dry land

All around our house
the sound of rain
making rivers

Taking a sour bite
I pass my son the apple
he gets the good side

Rabbit in the driveway
the headlights make it hop

Zigzagging
up the driveway
wearing wet fur

Bricks shined on by rain
a raven calling from the woods

A break in the weather
the branches jeweled
with rain

Everyone who sees it
points at the rainbow

Shadows appear
on the yellow wall
the sun is out

Birds stand out
on the bare branches

A familiar feeling
walking by a cedar
green reaching down

Rolled up sleeves
arms disappearing
into pumpkin

Before I cook breakfast
tip the frying pan
let the spider out

For a moment
the moon shows
in the window

Sleepy morning
imagine diving into
that plowed field

The clouds open
a circle around the moon

This winding walk
steep as a mountain
we know where to go

On the hill above town
begging door to door
trick or treating

Naturally
our son chose wisely
who to be

Perfect costume
to be someone
everyone wants to help

Out of sight
I hear their door open
"Charlie Brown!"

People know his story
a feeling of compassion
when they see him

Walking, walking
with only a bag
stopping to beg

We know houses
by the light of pathways
candles lead to doors

Holding out a bowl
whatever falls in
that will do

A pilgrim
with only a bowl
and poetry

LIFE IN THE RAIN

1.
In the Spring rain again
everything is green and growing.
The lampposts are budding all over
vines that blossom little bulbs
soon will be twinkling
pale light along the street.
That's how I see it
from my chair on the porch
writing poetry at night.
That's my job
believe it or not.
The poems provide
enough to pay rent
about as much money
as the flowers make light.

2.
After a long winter
it just rains and rains.
It's like living in a cloud
as if a raincloud descended
and people built their town
inside of it, living their lives
fogbound and floating.
Carved within the water
I just observe the rain
and write about the weather.

3.
The weather is everything
a constant topic of conversation
anything else can wait.
In fact our newspaper
makes it their motto
"Yesterday's News Tomorrow."
I had a conversation with
my neighbor who works there.
They have it all figured out.
They're doing us a favor
by slowing us down
keeping us out of the moment.
It's no accident they deliver
their words on hoop-wheel bicycle
the slower the better is their refrain
as if the rain has rusted them
and news is nothing that can't wait.
At least their weather predictions
are always right: rain, rain, rain.

4.
So what is it like anyway
to hold a week of rain
cupped in your hands?
Since people might be reading this
who live in deserts or on the moon
here, let me tell you:

Wednesday

I woke up to the little bird
in the can beside my bed.
After a warm shower
I held a pan out the window
to get enough water for tea.

Thursday

You've got to be very quiet
step on no twigs searching for them.
Somewhere there are sand dollars
hiding in this morning.
But I was reading a book
holding wet pages
and I forgot to look.

Friday

With feet of sparkling flying fish
see how she moves and hovers
at puddles in the rain.
The fish give her power
there's no need to ask her
how she floats on the air.

Saturday

Oh, that's not rain
there's a big watering can
high above the house.
Come outside, look
you can see the tree
holding the handle.

Sunday

Featuring the chickadees
the pat of rain on leaves
and below are soft footsteps
my boots in wet mud.

Monday

All night the dragon
flapped up and down
the street, perching on
a rooftop now and then
to blast out wind while
every fang-toothed fir tree
snapped at the sky.

Tuesday

By now we're used to it
We live in it like goldfish
When I go to work at dawn
I use the rain as stairs
walking up them through doors
down hallways and up more stairs
and someday I'll just keep on going.

Wednesday

A week of rain
the ground as soft as
clouds to walk upon

5.
I should describe the place
where I live, since most our life
is spent inside shelter.
That's usually how
stories are written, right?
Otherwise you might picture
something that isn't here
like me in a submarine
or some such thing.

6.
I don't live in a submarine
though it feels like we do.
Me, my wife and children
live in a leaning, cardboard
two story house painted green.
Most houses in the neighborhood
are painted gray or variations
on a rainy day.
In front there's the porch.
You already know about that.
Behind the house is overgrown
there's a boat in the backyard.
Most people try to keep one
just in case it gets real bad
and the water takes over.
Ours is a black sailboat
where a cat and her kittens
live in a sail in the bow.

7.
Weeds surround the boat
an impenetrable tangle
tall grass and a couple old
apple tree reminders of an orchard.
From there the Douglas firs start
becoming the forest going on
north to the white mountain.
Sometimes I see a deer or two.
I don't go back of the house much.
I like sitting on the porch
where I do my work.
The front yard isn't much
a slope of rain covered grass
that reaches the sidewalk
and our mailbox standing
beside the road.

8.
Usually all I get are bills
or advertisements that melt
once they touch my hand.
But sometimes I find
something else instead:

Hello,
This package of Sea Monkeys
was delivered by mistake to me.
As you can tell the box is
in pretty bad shape.
I don't know if anything is left inside.
Maybe you can write for a refund?

Sincerely,
Your next door neighbor

p.s. I did notice a lot of Sea Monkeys
living in my garden. They're on the leaves
making castles. If you want, we could
try to catch them.

9.
I know someone
who turned into a fish.
It happened like this.
Arthur lives next door.
I didn't know him that well.
I said hello a few times.
He nodded back.
Sometimes I saw him going
to work or coming home.
Eventually, the monotony
or all this endless rain
must have got to him.
He stood out in it
composed as a statue
with his clothes wet as leaves
and his skin cold as marble.
Our window in the kitchen
gave an aquarium view of
his not-so-slow transformation.
Like a koi in a pond, he moved
around, along the edge of the yard
bristling past rhododendron
pausing beneath the bare apple tree.
I suppose he stayed out there all night too.
At daylight, I went to check on him.

He was adrift in the uncut grass
laying on his back silently
staring at the drops falling down.
His shoes were torn off
body rigid, arms to his side
legs drawn long tight together.
He looked like an eel poured out
on the lawn. "Arthur…" I called.
I was wearing slippers, my feet
already soaked before I got to him.
"Arthur, are you okay?" He was.
I don't mean to worry you.
It's just that he was changed.
You couldn't miss it
not from where I stood.

Arthur had gills.
Sometimes it happens.
It's not unusual.
After months of rain
the daffodils show up
the tulips and dandelions
by the creek skunk cabbages grow.
People change too. It's natural.
Arthur made himself at home
in the fountain where he still
pilots himself about like a whale.

10.
One raining night, my daughter called
She was rehearsing a play at school
and her part called for her to wear
19th Century clothes and use an
English accent, awkward as a parasol.
I was the only one at home
I had no car so I went to the garage
and found other transportation.
Riding my bicycle took about five minutes
hissing wheels to get to her. I stopped
beside her and she hopped on back.
She told me about the shortcut
through the woods behind school.
Little did I know that when we left
the pavement, we seemed to leave
this century too.

The dirt path was unlit
I had to go slow and sense where
there might be holes or roots of trees.
She squeaked behind me and once
we dropped and slid off the path.
That's when I decided to stop
so we could walk instead.
The rain came and went
as it wanted to, the sky was a room
in a house with bad plumbing.
The rain puddles washed our feet
and the branches told us when
we were off course. She said
we were almost through the woods
to the paved road on the other side
when we heard the tiny sound of bells
like a village in the mountains
sheltered by hands of snow.

Someone was approaching us
using a staff with a lantern at the top.
The sound arrived with a glowing
green light that got so bright
we had to shield our eyes.
The air trembled with wings
you could feel them on your skin
as he led all those moths past us
along the path and into the night.

11.
One morning we had a great idea.
After breakfast we took our dishes
plates and spoons out into the yard
laying them down all around
for the rain to fall upon
and make sound.
It got better as time went on
as cups filled, bowls drummed.
By evening they were all in tune
The Rain Song Orchestra
playing us to sleep.

12.
*"It's entirely possible that all this rain
is actually the insidious weapon of
one of America's many enemies.
Afghanistan, Pakistan, China, Iran…
the list goes on and on…
Couldn't someone over there
be responsible for all our rain,
these wet bombs pounding us
day after day, breaking down
our defenses and our mental and
physical health? It's conceivable
we could be in a race to control
the weather. If so, we are woefully
unprepared and at the mercy of—"*

*Radio broadcast overheard at 6:24 A.M.

13.
I don't know why
there's one raindrop that won't fall.
It stays hovered right above
the railing on the balcony.
It's been suspended there
for quite a while, never changing
it remains a teardrop shape
only inches from reaching its end.
I can get right up to it and stare
into it like a little ball of glass.
I wish I could look deeper into it.
There's probably a world of water
in there we don't even know.

14.
The last job I had showed me
what it means to live in poverty.
Every morning I joined a work crew
assembled at some prearranged spot in town.
We got a shovel and were directed
where to dig and when.
Because of all the rainfall
the town is always on the point of
washing away. As a result
we need to dig channels everyday
so the water can flow to the sea.
Where the channels are dug
comes down to simple economics.
If you can't afford to pay the Channel Fee
you'll find a river running through
where you live. Some people are willing
to put up with that. There are even those
who have their homes raised up on stilts
so they don't have to pay at all.

For most people though
if you don't have the fifty bucks a month
you'll soon find yourself drowning.
Back when I wasn't making a living
as a poet, I was barely making ends meet
and it wasn't uncommon for
that bill to go a little late.
One time I couldn't come up
with the cash and for a while
the stairs became a waterfall.
I had to fight up the current.
Hand over hand holding to the rail
nailed to the wall, I made my way.
I was so tired when I got to the top
I stood in the flat rush of water
and didn't notice the salmon
in the cuff of my trousers.

15.
The rainy air is a sort of ocean.
I watched as a man paddled a rowboat
over my house. He just cleared the rooftop
and almost hit the chimney, pushing away
with his oar. He kept going, swinging those oars
out like bird wings, over the yards and trees
towards the aqueduct, aiming for a space
between the tall stone pillars.

16.
The early morning birds woke the day.
There were the tracks of a wheeled bathtub
bent into the grass, going around the garden.
The Mermaid had been by last night again.
I thought I heard her. Sometimes
she sings the saddest sound
like a mourning dove.

17.
You wouldn't expect to see
a piano pushed in the rain
like a tall black ship
shining along the sidewalk.
It was steered by two comedians.
They both wore bowler hats.
I've seen them around.
Oliver Hardy in blue overalls
with his thin shadow Stan Laurel.
As they heaved the piano along
it would swivel ominously
a force at work they had no
business trying to control.
They had to try though
this was just the sort of thing
that defined them.
From my porch
I could hear Ollie yowl
and chide his partner
and I couldn't help laughing.

They were so doomed at their job
they were turning it into a wonder.
After Stan ran the piano into Ollie
and pinned him with an "Oof!"
into the cold bare trunk of a tree
their act had reached its end.
The piano was too much for
Stan alone and it clattered away.
It looked like it had the whole town
to roam as long as the incline allowed.
It would roll and pick up speed
roaring on its wheels forever.
I watched it shoot off the curb
at the end of the block
where it crashed into another piano
coming up the hill, pushed by
three other comedians I know
Curly, Larry and Moe.

18.
Author's note:
For a few days, it got sunny
so I didn't write. I didn't want
anything else but rain on these pages.
But now I understand, it's okay
the season is nearing its end.

19.
Outside, laying down
inside of a parked car
I'm listening to the rain fall
on the roof like a sewing machine
stitching a tin blanket overhead.
It's a nice sound, lulling.
As I go into it deeper
the raindrops don't seem
to be hitting randomly.
Now I picture a typewriter.
There's a pattern to the sound
if only I had time and
the peace of mind
I'm sure I could keep track.
The message would reveal
like Morse code tapped out,
telling me something important
about life in the rain.

20.
The next new day
it happened all at once.
The gray clouds were lifted
out of the way and the sun
made the world yellow.
It didn't take long
maybe a minute at the most
before every tree was filled
with birds playing radio.
It's a different feeling
now the sun is here.
easy to forget all that
rain and cold weather.
Far away as childhood
poured from a bucket
as all the rain is gone
down drains, gutters
aqueducts to the sea.

Puddles are dry
it happened so easily.
Sitting here in sunshine
all the world is warm
my poetry is done
I'm half-asleep
and closing my eyes.

AIR TRAVEL:
10/21/11 begun 7 A.M on bus ride to job
until 11/2/11 in woods on break at job

OCTOBER WATER:
Written the month of October 2014

LIFE IN THE RAIN:
Written March—April 2012

Other Books by the Author

Ohio Trio (Bottom Dog Press 2001)

Bowl of Water (Bottom Dog Press 2003)

Another Life (Bird Dog Publishing 2007)

Home Recordings (Bird Dog Publishing 2009)

The Mermaid Translation (Bird Dog Publishing 2010)

The Selected Correspondence of Kenneth Patchen edited by Allen Frost (Bottom Dog Press 2012)

The Wonderful Stupid Man (Bird Dog Publishing 2012)

Saint Lemonade (Good Deed Rain 2014)

Playground (Good Deed Rain 2014)

Roosevelt (Good Deed Rain, 2015)

5 Novels (Good Deed Rain, 2015)

The Sylvan Moore Show (Good Deed Rain 2015)

Kirkus Review
ROOSEVELT
Frost, Allen Illus. by Sodt, Fred Good Deed Rain (174 pp.) $11.56 paperback ISBN: 978-1-933964-88-1; January 29, 2015

In this novel for middle-grade readers, a Pacific Northwestern boy searches for an escaped circus elephant with help from his eccentric uncle and a friend.

It's 1942 in Bellingham, Washington, and the circus is coming to town. At the fairground, fourth-grader George is dazzled by the lights, noise, and excitement—"every sense was boiling, a million times over." Even so, George "wondered how it would be for an animal," like Roosevelt the elephant. That night, he dreams of Roosevelt escaping and finds that it's true when he returns to the now-empty circus fairground. A circus clown left behind to search for Roosevelt (who has a habit of getting loose) gives George an elephant calling horn so he can look. Meanwhile, George's brother Andrew has just been called up to the Army, and the town makes homefront preparations. With his friend Kristine and some supernatural aid from his uncle Robert, George helps Roosevelt, while Andrew makes his own escape. With his fine, poetic imagery, Frost (5 Novels, 2015, etc.) captures the magic not just of the circus, but of friendship, animals, summer days, and special moments: "The clicking clacking of the railroad tracks sewed up the night"; "music, laughter and voices linked together like a paperclip chain tied from house to house." Characterization is deft and effective, as when George notices an aphid on Kristine's arm and likes "the way she noticed it too and put her fingertip near it, and let it climb on so she could give it a big leaf to live on." Though Uncle Robert's magical solution is too easy, he's an interesting figure, with his top hat and daytime moviegoing. Frost also ably brings in historical details, as when a showoff kid skids his bike wheels and George isn't impressed: "Everyone knew you weren't supposed to waste rubber."

Delightful, with appealing characters and a serious edge.

www.ingramcontent.com/pod-product-compliance
Lightning Source LLC
LaVergne TN
LVHW040102080526
838202LV00045B/3739